AF884978

Data & AI Strategy:
From Roadmap to Implementation

Colophon

Title: Data & AI Strategy: From Roadmap to Implementation

Authors: Victor de Graaff

Publisher: Van Haren Publishing, 's-Hertogenbosch

ISBN Paperback: 978 94 018 1267 2

Edition: First edition, first print, December, 2024

Design: Van Haren Publishing, 's-Hertogenbosch

For further information about Van Haren Publishing please e-mail us at: info@vanharen.net or visit our website: www.vanharen.net

Publisher about the Courseware

The Courseware was created by experts from the industry who served as the author(s) for this publication. The input for the material is based on existing publications and the experience and expertise of the author(s). The material has been revised by trainers who also have experience working with the material. Close attention was also paid to the key learning points to ensure what needs to be mastered.

The objective of the courseware is to provide maximum support to the trainer and to the student, during his or her training. The material has a modular structure and according to the author(s) has the highest success rate should the student opt for examination. The Courseware is also accredited for this reason, wherever applicable.

In order to satisfy the requirements for accreditation the material must meet certain quality standards. The structure, the use of certain terms, diagrams and references are all part of this accreditation. Additionally, the material must be made available to each student in order to obtain full accreditation. To optimally support the trainer and the participant of the training assignments, practice exams and results are provided with the material.

Direct reference to advised literature is also regularly covered in the sheets so that students can find additional information concerning a particular topic. The decision to leave out notes pages from the Courseware was to encourage students to take notes throughout the material.

Although the courseware is complete, the possibility that the trainer deviates from the structure of the sheets or chooses to not refer to all the sheets or commands does exist. The student always has the possibility to cover these topics and go through them on their own time. It is recommended to follow the structure of the courseware and publications for maximum exam preparation.

The courseware and the recommended literature are the perfect combination to learn and understand the theory.

-- Van Haren Publishing

Other publications by Van Haren Publishing

Van Haren Publishing (VHP) specializes in titles on Best Practices, methods and standards within four domains:

- IT and IT Management
- Architecture (Enterprise and IT)
- Business Management and
- Project Management

Van Haren Publishing is also publishing on behalf of leading organizations and companies: ASLBiSL Foundation, BRMI, CA, Centre Henri Tudor, Gaming Works, IACCM, IAOP, IFDC, Innovation Value Institute, IPMA-NL, ITSqc, NAF, KNVI, PMI-NL, PON, The Open Group, The SOX Institute.

Topics are (per domain):

IT and IT Management
ABC of ICT
ASL®
CATS CM®
CMMI®
COBIT®
e-CF
ISO/IEC 20000
ISO/IEC 27001/27002
ISPL
IT4IT®
IT-CMF™
IT Service CMM
ITIL®
MOF
MSF
SABSA
SAF
SIAM™
TRIM
VeriSM™

Enterprise Architecture
ArchiMate®
GEA®
Novius Architectuur
Methode
TOGAF®

Business Management
BABOK® Guide
BiSL® and BiSL® Next
BRMBOK™
BTF
EFQM
eSCM
IACCM
ISA-95
ISO 9000/9001
OPBOK
SixSigma
SOX
SqEME®

Project Management
A4-Projectmanagement
DSDM/Atern
ICB / NCB
ISO 21500
MINCE®
M_o_R®
MSP®
P3O®
PMBOK® Guide
Praxis®
PRINCE2®

For the latest information on VHP publications, visit our website: www.vanharen.net.

Table of content

Self-Reflection of understanding Diagram

'What you do not measure, you cannot control.'' – Tom Peters

Fill in this diagram to self-evaluate your understanding of the material. This is an evaluation of how well you know the material and how well you understand it. In order to pass the exam successfully you should be aiming to reach the higher end of Level 3. If you really want to become a pro, then you should be aiming for Level 4. Your overall level of understanding will naturally follow the learning curve. So, it's important to keep track of where you are at each point of the training and address any areas of difficulty.

Based on where you are within the Self-Reflection of Understanding diagram you can evaluate the progress of your own training.

Level of Understanding	*Before Training (Pre-knowledge)*	*Training Part 1 (1st Half)*	*Training Part 2 (2nd Half)*	*After studying / reading the book*	*After exercises and the Practice exam*
Level 4 *I can explain the content and apply it .*					
Level 3 *I get it!* *I am right where I am supposed to be.*					Ready for the exam!
Level 2 *I almost have it but could use more practice.*					
Level 1 *I am learning but don't quite get it yet.*					

(Self-Reflection of Understanding Diagram)

Write down the problem areas that you are still having difficulty with so that you can consolidate them yourself, or with your trainer. After you have had a look at these, then you should evaluate to see if you now have a better understanding of where you actually are on the learning curve.

Troubleshooting

Problem areas: *Topic:*

Part 1

Part 2

You have gone through the book and studied.

You have answered the questions and done the practice exam.

Timetable

Day 1: Foundation & Roadmap

- Introduction to Data & AI Strategy
- Creating the Fundamentals
- Developing a Roadmap
- Hands-on Workshop

Day 2: Implementation and Stakeholder Engagement

- First Steps in Implementation
- Engaging Stakeholders
- Establishing Insights
- Planning for Next Steps
- Hands-on Workshop

Day 3: Leveraging AI Tools for Business Efficiency

- Introduction to AI Tools in Business
- Hands-on Workshop with ChatGPT
- Deep Dive into Generative AI integration into your business
- Developing an Implementation Plan
- Next Steps and Q&A

Data & AI Strategy
from Roadmap to Implementation

Effective DATA Foundation
GENERATIVE AI AMBASSADOR
Certified by Van Haren

COURSEWARE

Van Haren PUBLISHING

Getting to know each other

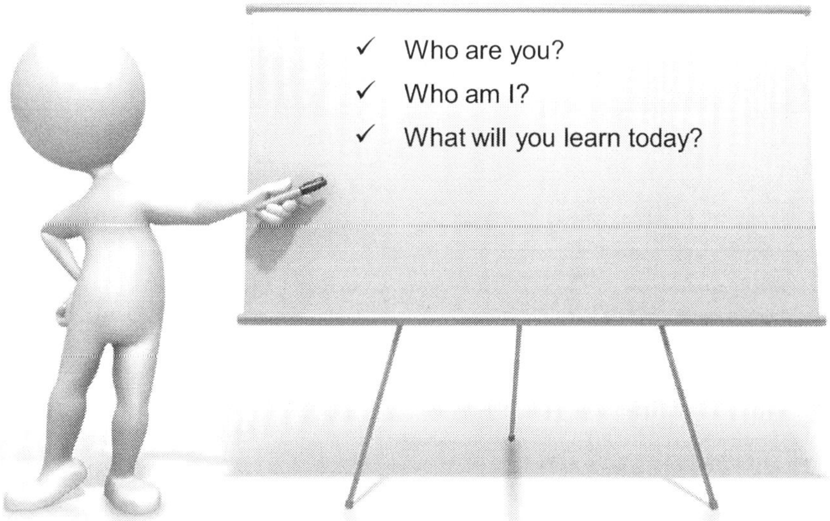

 2

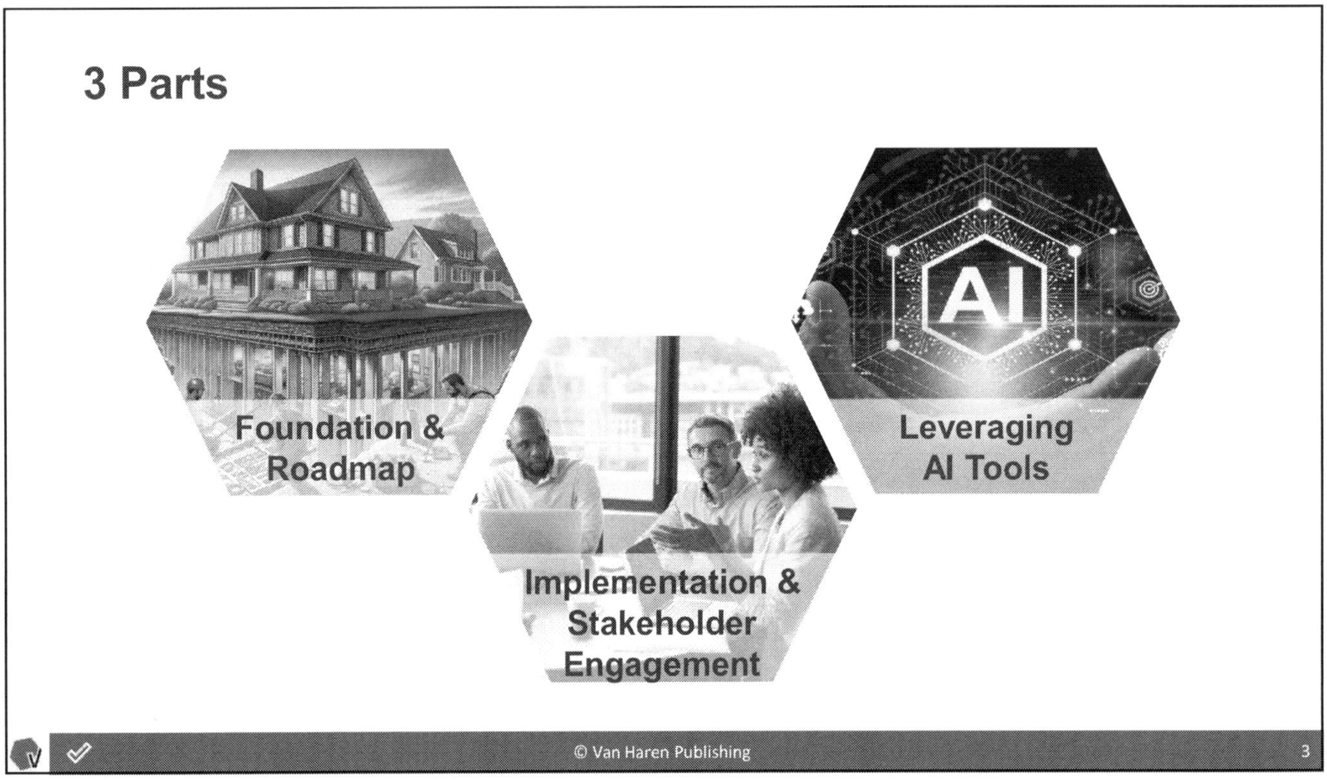
3 Parts
Foundation & Roadmap
Implementation & Stakeholder Engagement
AI
Leveraging AI Tools
© Van Haren Publishing
3

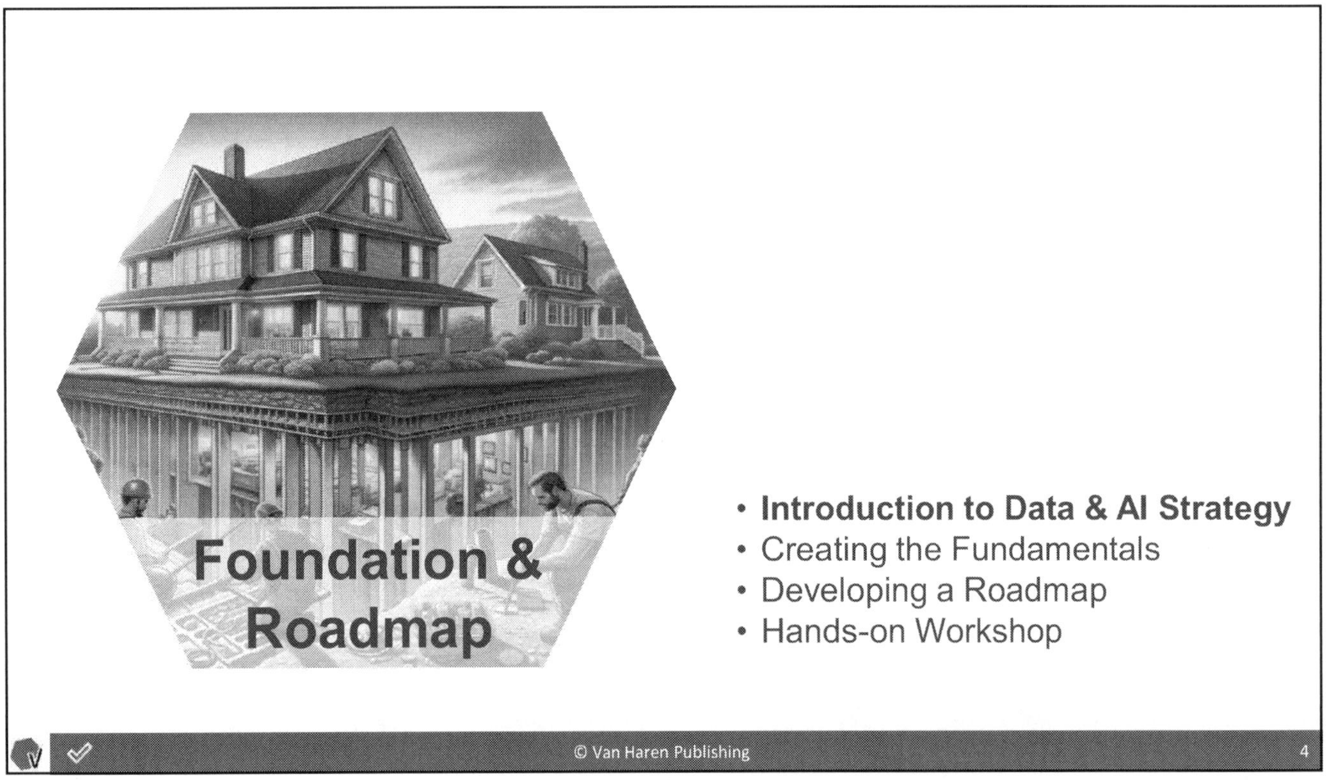
Foundation & Roadmap
• Introduction to Data & AI Strategy
• Creating the Fundamentals
• Developing a Roadmap
• Hands-on Workshop
© Van Haren Publishing
4

Introduction to Data & AI Strategy

- ✓ Overview of Data and AI in the business context
- ✓ Key components of a Data and AI strategy
- ✓ Importance of aligning Data and AI strategy with business goals

 5

"Good data is our number one goal!"

 6

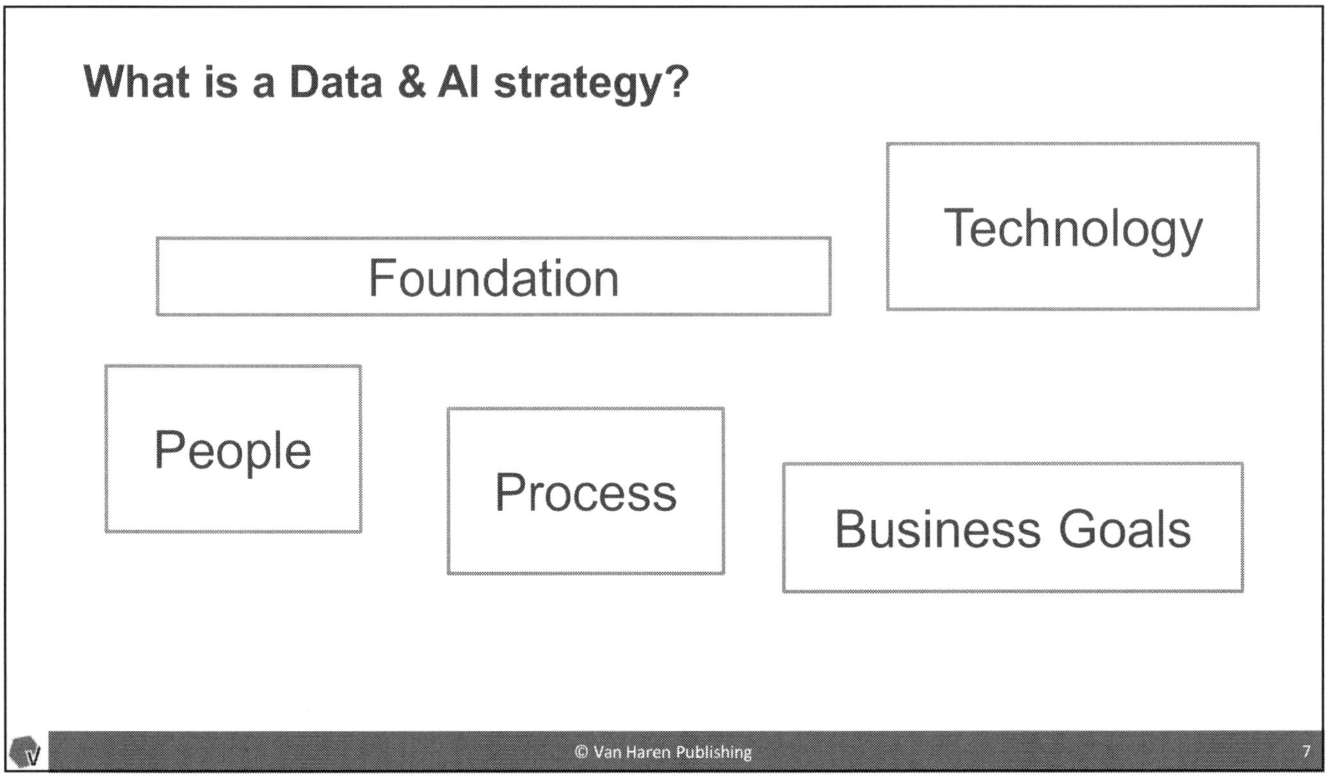
What is a Data & AI strategy?
Technology
Foundation
People
Process
Business Goals
© Van Haren Publishing
7

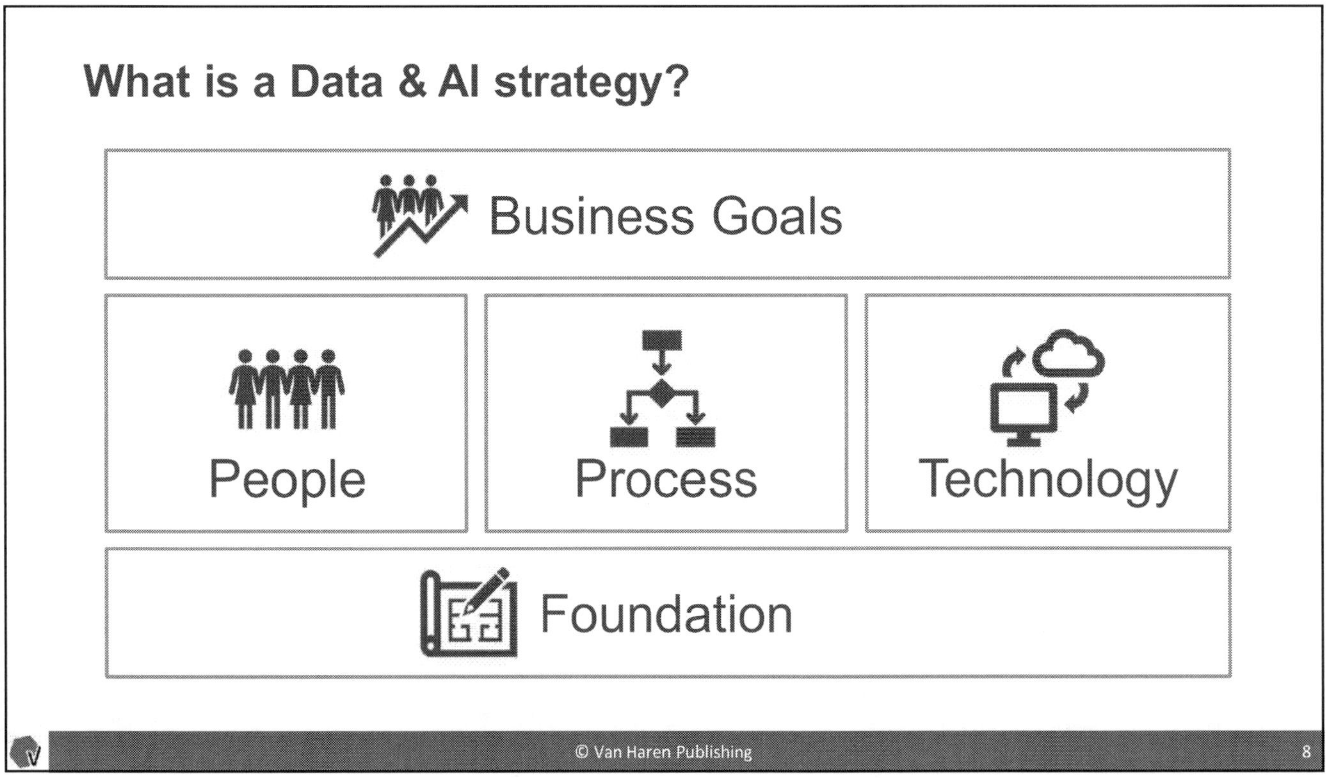
What is a Data & AI strategy?
Business Goals
People
Process
Technology
Foundation
© Van Haren Publishing
8

Business Goals

Understand your business goals.

Ask your stakeholders:

- ✓ Their top business goals that require data and AI use
- ✓ Biggest challenges
- ✓ Data privacy & security
- ✓ Time spent on data integration
- ✓ Data desires
- ✓ Success metrics

https://www.ibm.com/think/insights/data-differentiator/data-driven-organization

 9

People

- ✓ Training:
  - Data literacy
  - Self-service BI
  - How to use AI
- ✓ Foster a data-driven culture:
  - Share successes
  - Set KPIs on data (quality) metrics
  - Assign data ownership
- ✓ Explain roles & responsibilities:
  - How will their job be impacted by data & AI usage?
  - Data governance
- ✓ New teams / roles?
  - Data engineers
  - Data analists
  - Data scientists

 10

Process

✓ What are the key processes in the organization?

✓ Which processes can benefit most from data?

✓ How much effort will it take to make these processes data driven?

✓ Organize brainstorm sessions with the stakeholders / process owners

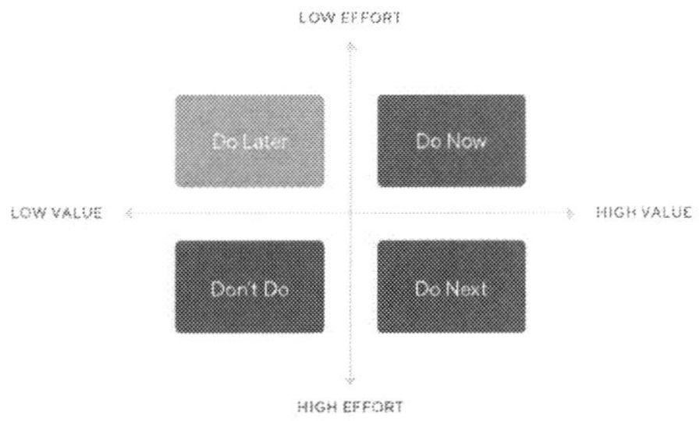

Technology

✓ "One" data platform

✓ But… different spaces on the platform

✓ Self-service:
- Give freedom, get results
- Analytical tooling
- Scripting

✓ Automate (meta-)data quality checks:
- Are golden standards followed?
- Does the data make sense?

Foundation

✓ Elements that impact all-of-the-above:
- Timelines
- Budgets
- (Legal) constraints

What is a Data & AI strategy?

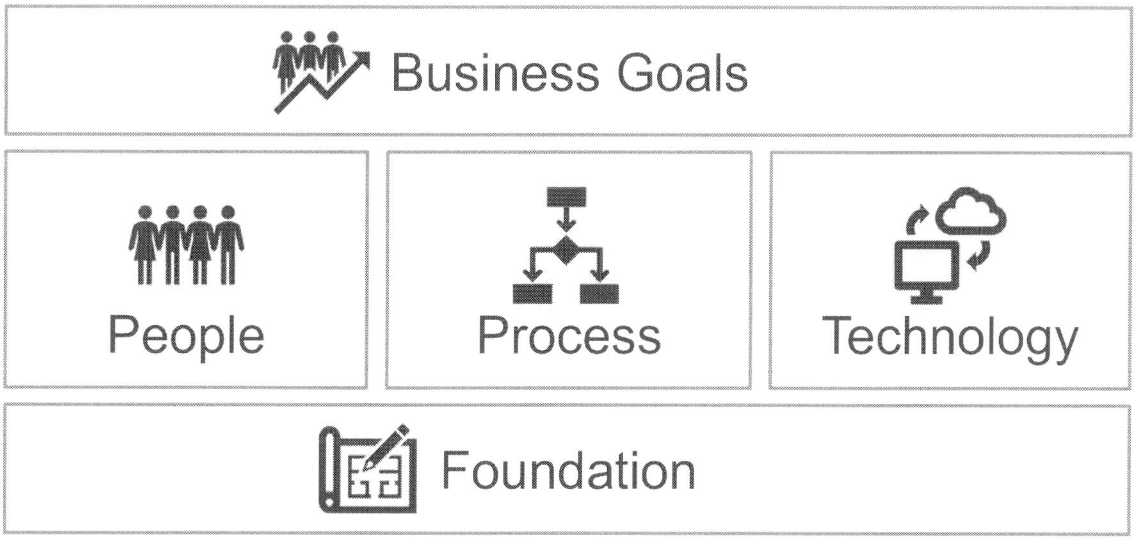

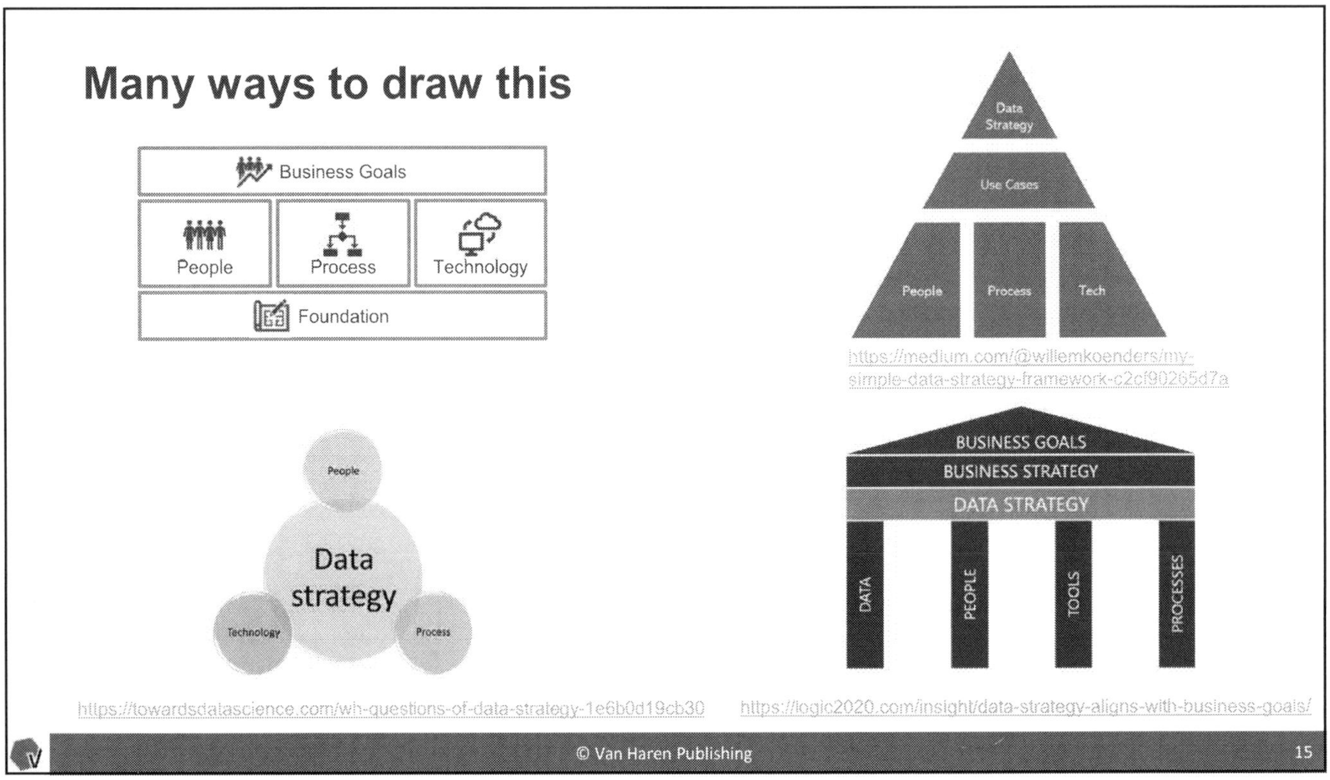
Many ways to draw this
Business Goals
People
Process
Technology
Foundation
Data Strategy
Use Cases
People
Process
Tech
https://medium.com/@willemkoenders/my-simple-data-strategy-framework-c2cf90265d7a
People
Data strategy
Technology
Process
BUSINESS GOALS
BUSINESS STRATEGY
DATA STRATEGY
DATA
PEOPLE
TOOLS
PROCESSES
https://towardsdatascience.com/wh-questions-of-data-strategy-1e6b0d19cb30
https://logic2020.com/insight/data-strategy-aligns-with-business-goals/
© Van Haren Publishing
15

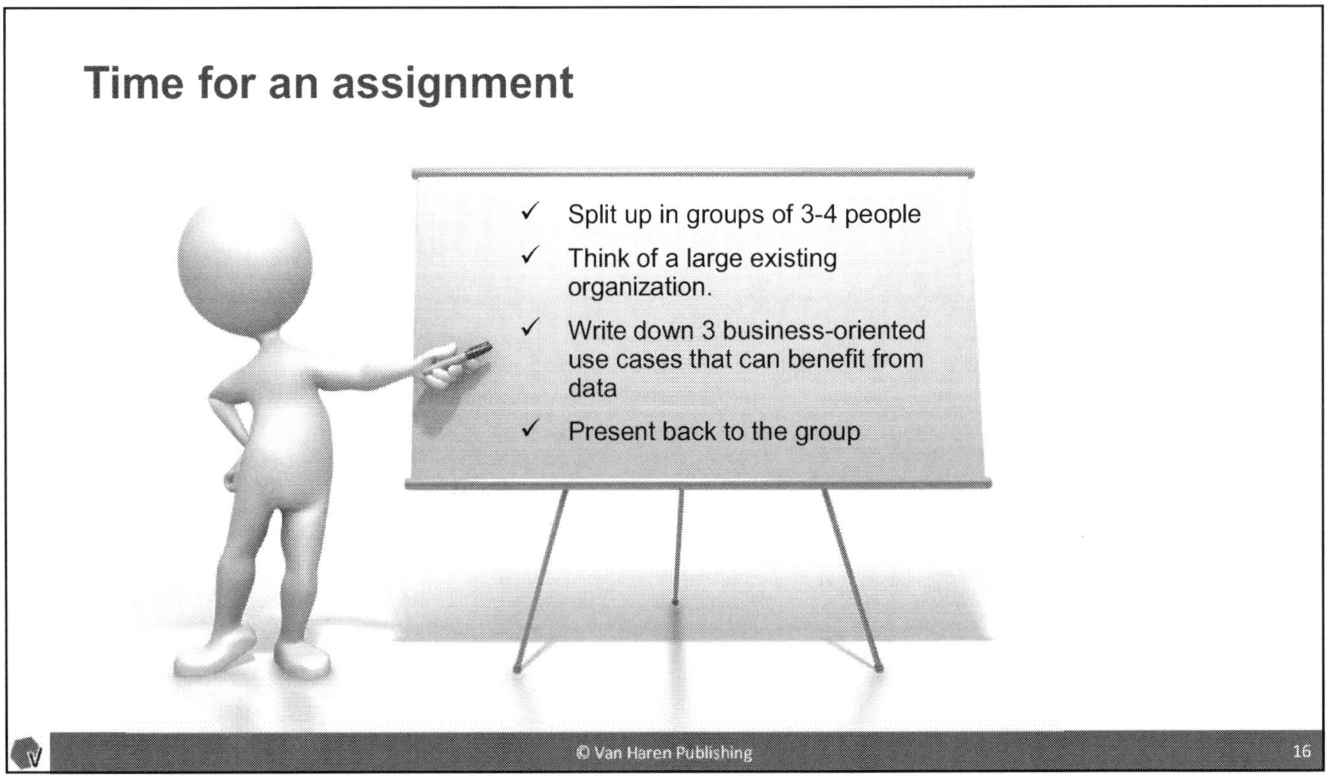
Time for an assignment
✓ Split up in groups of 3-4 people
✓ Think of a large existing organization.
✓ Write down 3 business-oriented use cases that can benefit from data
✓ Present back to the group
© Van Haren Publishing
16

- Introduction to Data & AI Strategy
- **Creating the Fundamentals**
- Developing a Roadmap
- Hands-on Workshop

 17

"All our data needs to be interoperable!"

 18

Key components of a good Data & AI Strategy

- ✓ Alignment with Business Objectives
- ✓ Analytics and Data Maturity Evaluation
- ✓ Data Architecture and Technology
- ✓ The Data Analytics Team
- ✓ Effective Data Governance
- ✓ Data Strategy Roadmap
- ✓ Culture Change and Adoption

https://www.analytics8.com/blog/7-elements-of-a-data-strategy/

 19

Key components: Alignment with Business Objectives

- ✓ Identify relevant business drivers — big or small — that could be positively impacted by data and analytics.
- ✓ Understand departmental activities and how they sync up with business goals.
- ✓ Interview:
  - Start at the executive level
  - Also department leaders
- ✓ Uncover:
  - Their goals
  - Day-to-day business
  - Potential improvements
  - What is being measured
  - Information needs
- ✓ Compare your findings to industry standards: did you miss something?

 20

Key components: Analytics and Data Maturity Evaluation

	Chaotic	Reactive	Defined	Managed	Optimized
	Teams are overwhelmed, lack confidence in reports and lack capacity for data-driven decision making.	Visibility on business' health is limited by reports that only offer a partial glimpse of past performance and lagging indicators.	Leaders have accurate data and defined key metrics shown within dashboards. They know what is happening today, and why.	Leaders have integrated enterprise analytics and cross- domain metrics that that provide some multi-faceted views and focus on future outcomes.	The organization is powered by enterprise analytics systems including predictive metrics, and data-driven decision making at all levels.
Analytics/ Reporting Structure	Nonexistent	Nonexistent	Basic/ Minimal	Integrated	Advanced
Analytics Management Processes	Siloed	Siloed	Siloed	Integrated	Governed
KPIs	Undefined and Ad-Hoc	Past Performance	Present/ Real-time	Measure Future Outcomes	Predictive and Comprehensive
Confidence in Data	Low	Partial	Partial	Full	Full
Employee Capabilities	Limited	Varied	Varied	Enabled	Enhanced

https://www.analytics8.com/blog/7-elements-of-a-data-strategy/

Data quality

- ✓ Accuracy
- ✓ Completeness
- ✓ Consistency
- ✓ Integrity
- ✓ Reasonableness
- ✓ Timeliness
- ✓ Uniqueness

DAMA International

Data usefulness

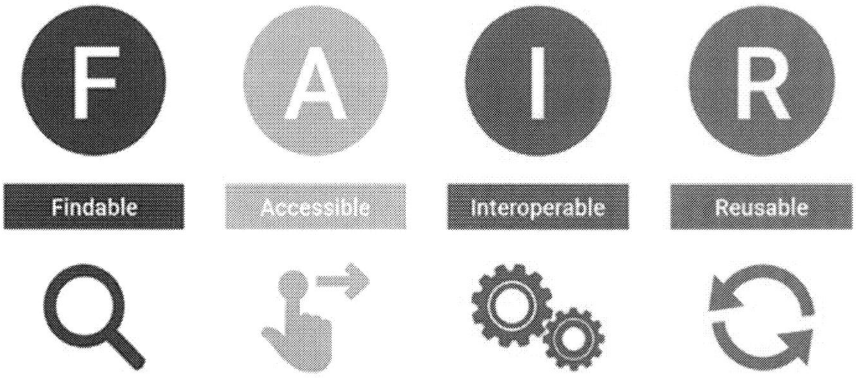

 23

Key components: Data Architecture and Technology

✓ Data architecture choices are tightly coupled with operations. Three design paradigms:
- Structure before storing: use a data warehouse (ETL)
- Store first, structure later: use a datalake (ELT)
- No central data duplication: use data mesh or data virtualization

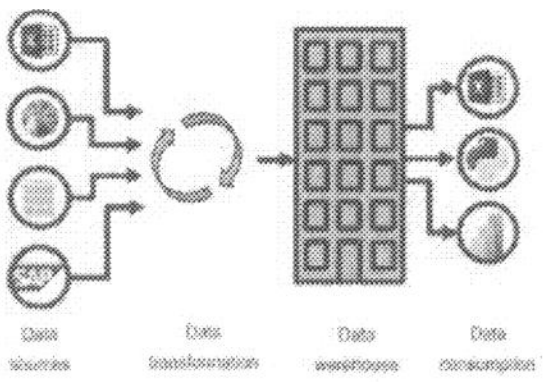

Extract-transform-load (ETL)

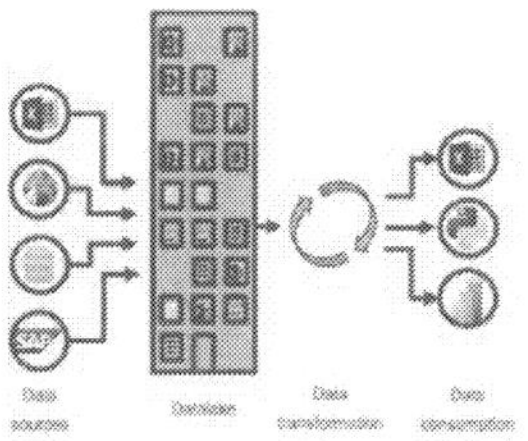

Extract-load-transform (ELT)

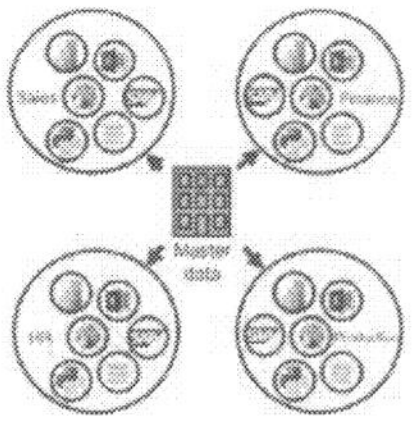

Data mesh

 24

Key components: The Data Analytics Team

- ✓ Team of mathematicians and computer scientists
- ✓ Complementary to the experts in the business lines
- ✓ Work in multi-disciplinary teams **with** domain experts on a project-basis
- ✓ Identifies business opportunities based on **available technology** in **collaboration** with domain experts

 25

Key components: Effective Data Governance

What is data governance?

- ✓ Framework for managing data assets effectively
- ✓ Ensures data accuracy, consistency, and security
- ✓ Aligns data management with business objectives
- ✓ Key to compliance with regulations and standards

 26

Key components: Effective Data Governance

Why is data governance important?

- ✓ Provides trust in data for decision-making
- ✓ Mitigates risks related to data misuse
- ✓ Supports regulatory compliance (e.g., GDPR)
- ✓ Enhances operational efficiency through better data

Key components: Effective Data Governance

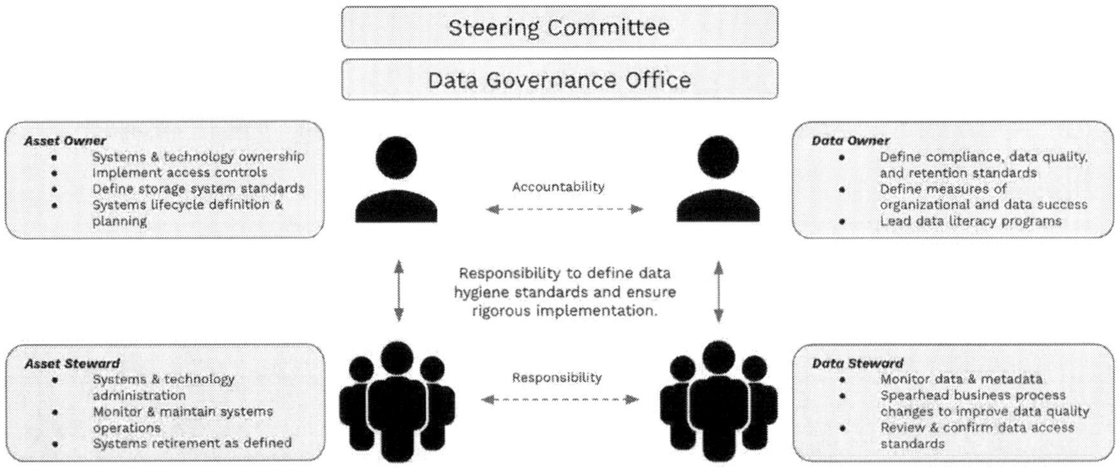

https://www.pythian.com/blog/business-insights/identifying-and-engaging-data-stewards

Key components: Effective Data Governance

Steps to implement data governance:

1. Define goals aligned with business needs
2. Identify and assign key roles and responsibilities
3. Establish data policies and standards
4. Implement tools for data management and monitoring
5. Continuously review and improve governance practices

 29

Key components: Data Strategy Roadmap

- ✓ Clearly define the current state
- ✓ Define which business goals are to be optimized, within a reasonable amount of time
- ✓ Identify dependencies, then plan the business goals on a timeline
- ✓ Understand that the involvement of certain roles changes over time:

Role	Proof-of-concept	MVP	Production
Data scientist	★★★	★★	★
Data engineer	★	★★	★★★
Domain expert	★★★	★★	★★★

more later…

 30

Key components: Culture Change and Adoption

"Improving daily work is even more important than doing daily work."

 31

Key components

- ✓ Alignment with Business Objectives
- ✓ Analytics and Data Maturity Evaluation
- ✓ Data Architecture and Technology
- ✓ The Data Analytics Team
- ✓ Effective Data Governance
- ✓ Data Strategy Roadmap
- ✓ Culture Change and Adoption

 32

Foundation & Roadmap

- Introduction to Data & AI Strategy
- Creating the Fundamentals
- **Developing a Roadmap**
- Hands-on Workshop

 33

Developing a Roadmap

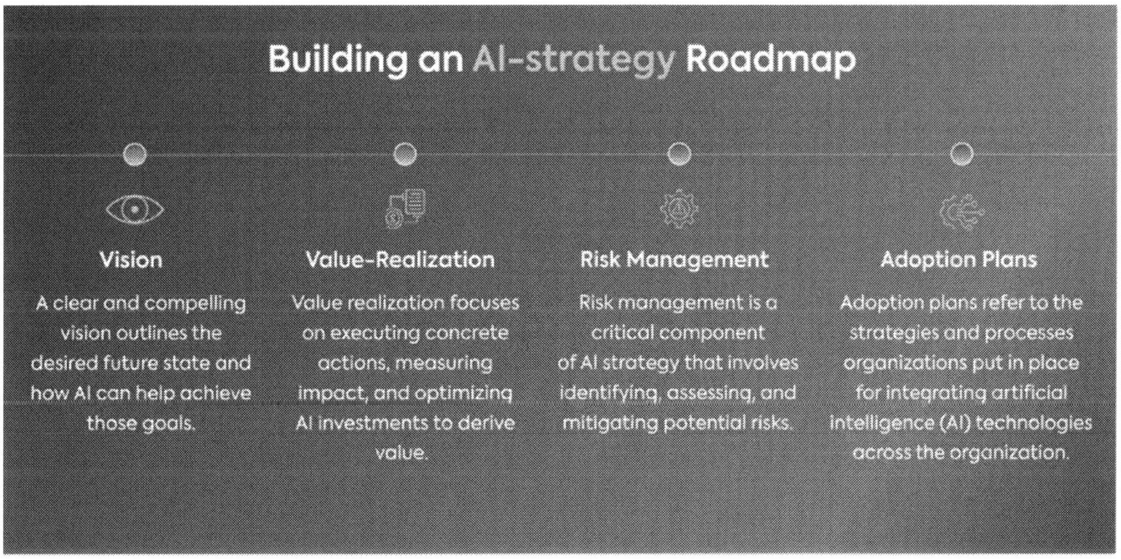

https://www.auxiliobits.com/how-to-drive-value-for-your-business-with-an-ai-strategy-roadmap/

 34

Vision

- ✓ Alignment with Business Objectives
- ✓ Long-Term Perspective
- ✓ Cross-Functional Collaboration
- ✓ Ethical and Responsible AI

 35

Value-realization

Remember: a KPI is **not** a goal

- ✓ Define Measurable Goals
- ✓ Establish Key Performance Indicators (KPIs)
- ✓ Data-Driven Decision Making
- ✓ Iterative Improvement
- ✓ Start with low-hanging fruit

 36

Risk Management

- ✓ Ethical Frameworks and Guidelines
- ✓ Regulatory Compliance
- ✓ Bias Detection and Mitigation
- ✓ Cybersecurity and Data Protection

 37

Adoption Plans

- ✓ Change Management
- ✓ Skill Development and Talent Acquisition
- ✓ Cross-Functional Collaboration
- ✓ Scalability and Sustainability
- ✓ User Experience Design
- ✓ Measurement and Feedback

Remember: a data scientist is not a change manager!

 38

- Introduction to Data & AI Strategy
- Creating the Fundamentals
- Developing a Roadmap
- **Hands-on Workshop**

 39

Assignment: build your own roadmap

- ✓ Split up in groups of 2-3
- ✓ Get paper & markers
- ✓ Split the paper in 4 pieces, each of the four pieces becomes one of the items:
  - ✓ Vision
  - ✓ Value-realization
  - ✓ Risk management
  - ✓ Adoption plans

4 x 5 minutes

 40

- Introduction to Data & AI Strategy
- Creating the Fundamentals
- Developing a Roadmap
- Hands-on Workshop

 41

3 Parts

 42

Implementation & Stakeholder Engagement

- **First Steps in Implementation**
- Engaging Stakeholders
- Establishing Insights
- Planning for Next Steps
- Hands-on Workshop

First steps in implementation: prioritize

✓ Set up brainstorm sessions inside the departments:
  - Which processes need improvement?
  - How much effort is needed to improve these processes?
  - Use the output from the interview sessions within that department as a starting point

✓ Use t-shirt sizes or a similar approach to estimate effort and value

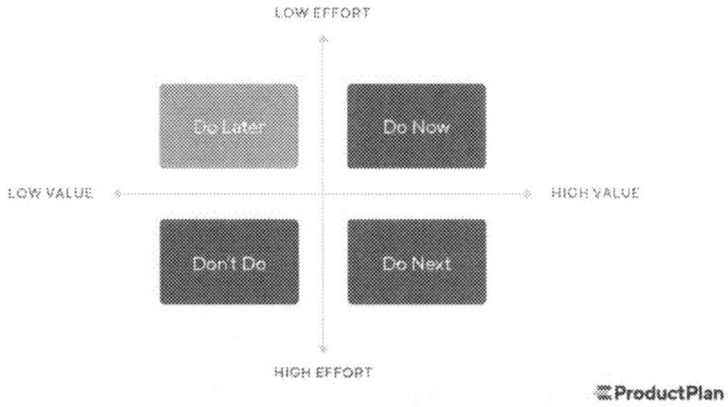

First steps in implementation: setting up the first BI / AI projects

- ✓ For the most promising cases, use a framework like CRISP-DM
- ✓ For BI projects, read “build the dashboard” instead of “modeling”

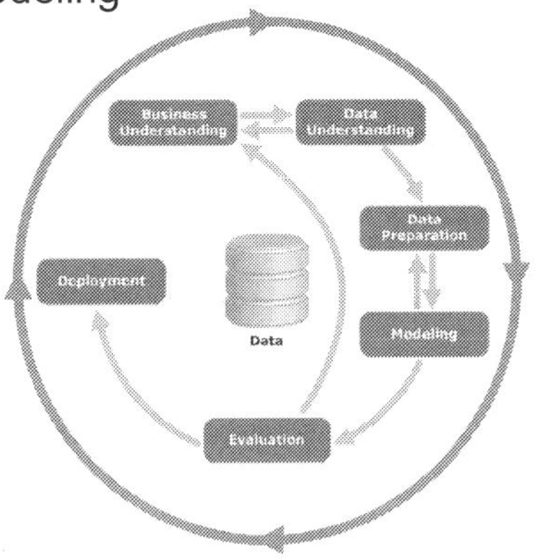

 45

Business understanding

Make sure you understand what the problem is:

- ✓ General problem description
- ✓ Vocabulary
- ✓ Stakeholders and their representatives
- ✓ Potential impact
- ✓ Definition of Done
- ✓ Key datasets

 46

Assignment: design a project plan for one AI use case

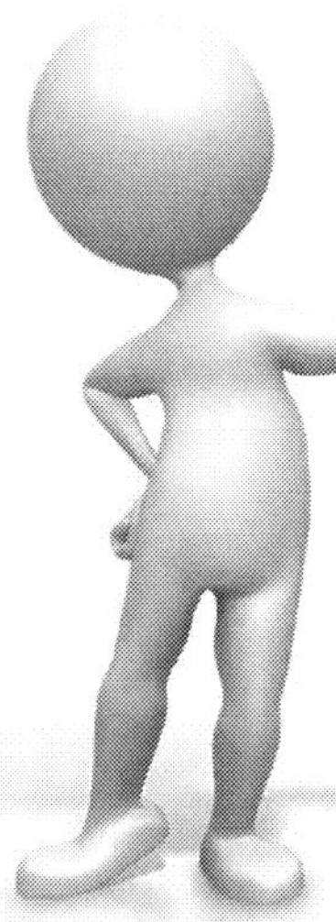

- ✓ Form groups of 3
- ✓ Come up with a use case for AI in your day-to-day job
- ✓ Fill out the intake form
- Check your problem description with your trainer before continuing, not every problem is an AI problem

- Problem description
- Vocabulary
- Stakeholders
- Potential impact
- Definition of Done
- Key datasets

 47

Data understanding: assess data quality

- ✓ For the most promising cases, assess the data quality:
  - Accuracy
  - Completeness
  - Consistency
  - Integrity
  - Reasonableness
  - Timeliness
  - Uniqueness
- ✓ Thomas Redman (aka "The Data Doc"):
  Print out 100 lines of data from each table

 48

Data preparation

- ✓ Combine data from multiple sources
- ✓ Visualize the data to understand if it makes sense
- ✓ Cross-check data over multiple sources: do they add up to the same numbers as in existing reports?
- ✓ Make sure data aggregates to the same level (time intervals, regions, etc)

 49

First steps in implementation: visualize data

Visualizing data is an easy way to:

- ✓ Assess data quality in further depth
- ✓ Understand the relation between different columns and tables

 50

Build the dashboard / model

- ✓ In this step AI and BI deviate the most from each other:
  - AI: build the model
  - BI: build the dashboard
- ✓ Let BI consultants build the dashboard, or data scientists do the modelling
- ✓ Make sure there are constant check-ins between the BI consultants / data scientists and the domain experts. This:
  - Avoids double work
  - Ensures the results actually bring the business goals closer
- ✓ Note: on a self-service platform, the domain expert and BI consultant may be the same person. This approach is not suitable for every organization.

 51

Evaluation

- ✓ Evaluate the model / report. If this goes live, will the business actually benefit?
  - What can be gained from the model / dashboard?
  - What is the price-to-pay if the model is wrong? (e.g. *false positives/negatives)*

 52

Deployment

- ✓ Deploy the dashboard / model
- ✓ When successful: scale up from PoC to MVP to productionized model/dashboard
- ✓ Ensure a team will maintain the model/dashboard. Either the team that built it or a specific team that monitors all models.
- ✓ Advantage of team that built it: knowing you will be the one maintaining the code, automatically improves the way-of-working

 53

Assignment: design a project plan for one AI use case

- ✓ Go back to your group of 3
- ✓ We re-use the challenge from the previous assignment
- ✓ Now complete the CRISP-DM cycle for the remaining steps:
  what will you need to do in each of the steps?

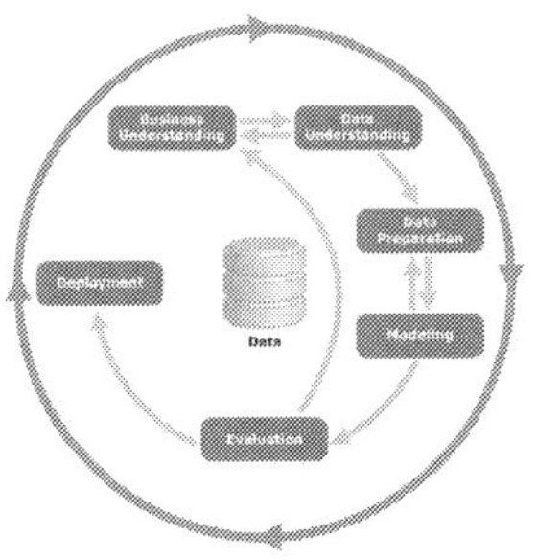

 54

Implementation &
Stakeholder
Engagement
• First Steps in Implementation
• **Engaging Stakeholders**
• Establishing Insights
• Planning for Next Steps
• Hands-on Workshop
© Van Haren Publishing
55

3 habits of engaging stakeholders
Train & Encourage
Assign ownership
Reward customers
© Van Haren Publishing
56

3 habits of engaging stakeholders

Train & Encourage

- Give people the space to experiment
- Work from trust, rather than from fear
- Explain & train people with new tools
- Share successes, especially with those who made them possible (eg. MDM team)
- Ensure a high level of *data literacy* within the teams

 57

3 habits of engaging stakeholders

Assign ownership

- Put people in charge of data assets:
    - Datasets
    - Dashboards
    - Models
- Train them on strategy & tools
- Explain how to measure quality
- Reward them for high quality
- Transform them into ambassadors

 58

Lay the Foundation for Success

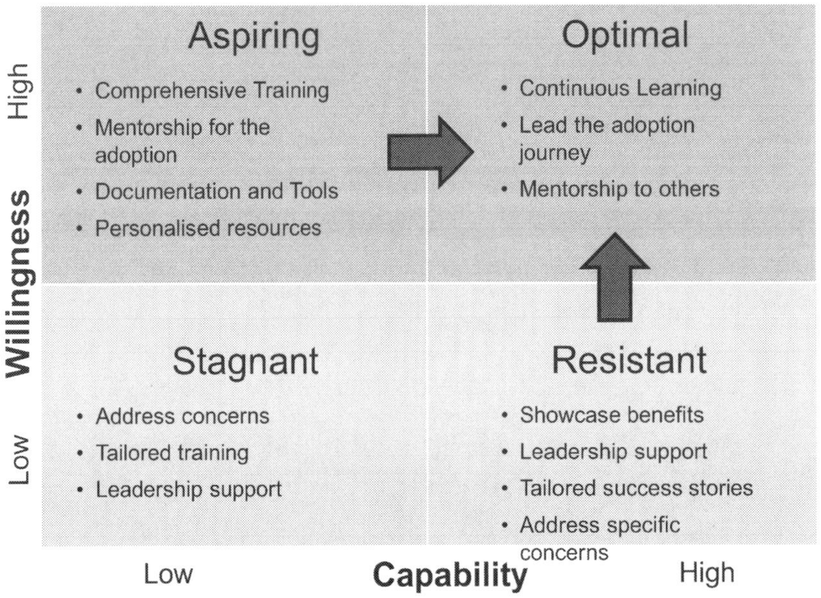

- Identifying the right champions in the organisation is key to a successful BIAN adoption and rollout
- However the optimal champions don't always exist
- How to create the right champions?

3 habits of engaging stakeholders

Reward customers

- Customers are the first point of data entry:
  - Address updates
  - Purchases
- Reward them for providing clean data:
  - Loyalty programs

3 habits of engaging stakeholders
Train & Encourage
Assign ownership
Reward customers
© Van Haren Publishing
61

Implementation & Stakeholder Engagement
• First Steps in Implementation
• Engaging Stakeholders
• Establishing Insights
• Planning for Next Steps
• Hands-on Workshop
© Van Haren Publishing
62

Establishing insights

- ✓ Create dashboards per business goal and show the respective KPIs
  - eg: sales of a specific department
- ✓ Create dashboards that will help to improve those KPIs
  - eg: up-selling opportunities
- ✓ Ensure the people who can benefit from these dashboards are actively monitoring these
- ✓ Leverage notable data points by **sorting** or **alerting** specific cases
- ✓ Use AI models to uncover relationships between your KPIs and actions from the past

Tools

- ✓ Use analytics platforms, such as Power BI, Tableau, QlikView, etc
- ✓ Integrate AI models into your dashboards, eg relating datapoints to benchmarks
- ✓ Utilize data pipelines for real-time updates
- ✓ Ensure scalability (eg using cloud technology)

Embedding Insights in Business Processes

- ✓ Align insights with operational workflows
- ✓ Automate decisions using AI-powered systems (when impact or risk is low enough)
- ✓ Enable cross-department collaboration on insights
- ✓ Regularly update models and reports for relevance

Ensuring Trust in Insights

- ✓ Maintain transparency in algorithms and predictions
- ✓ Provide training for stakeholders to interpret insights
- ✓ Continuously monitor data quality and performance

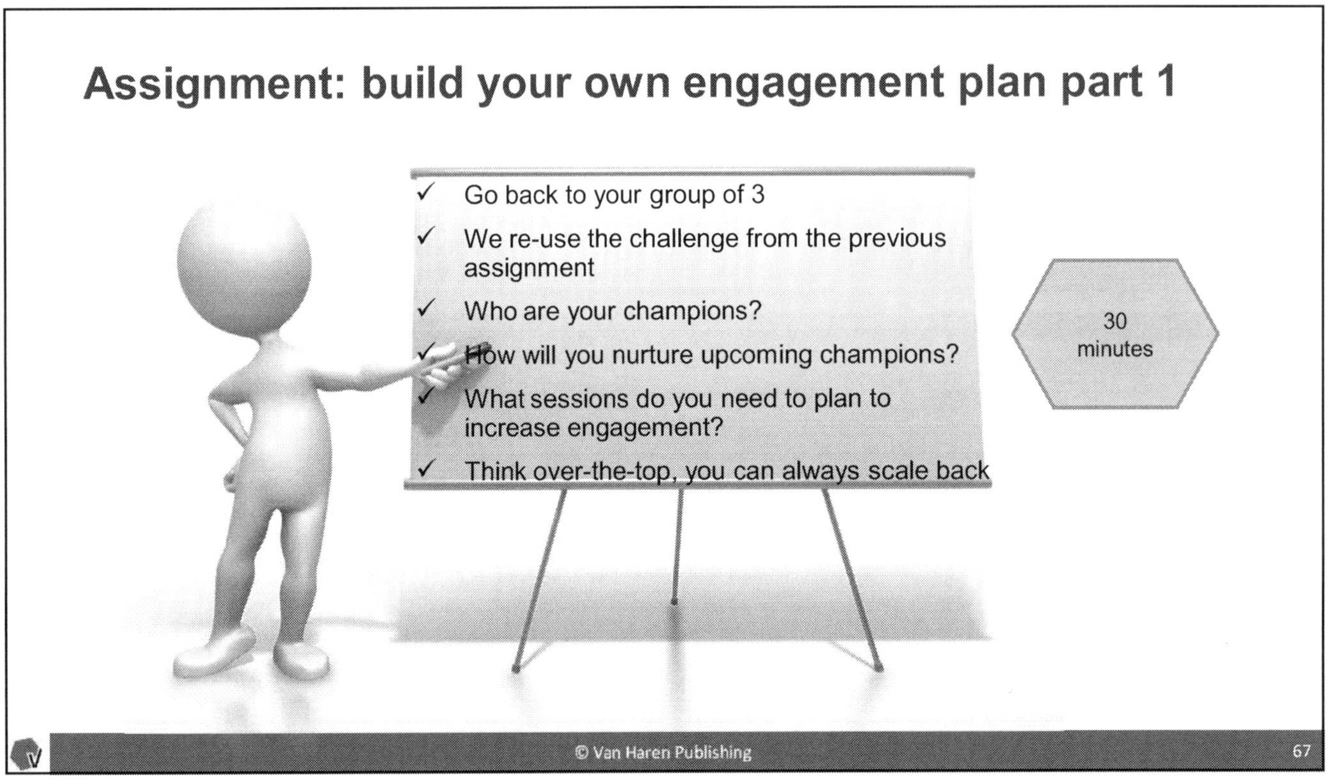
Assignment: build your own engagement plan part 1
✓ Go back to your group of 3
✓ We re-use the challenge from the previous assignment
✓ Who are your champions?
✓ How will you nurture upcoming champions?
✓ What sessions do you need to plan to increase engagement?
✓ Think over-the-top, you can always scale back
30 minutes
© Van Haren Publishing
67

Implementation & Stakeholder Engagement
• First Steps in Implementation
• Engaging Stakeholders
• Establishing Insights
• Planning for Next Steps
• Hands-on Workshop
© Van Haren Publishing
68

Different stages of maturity

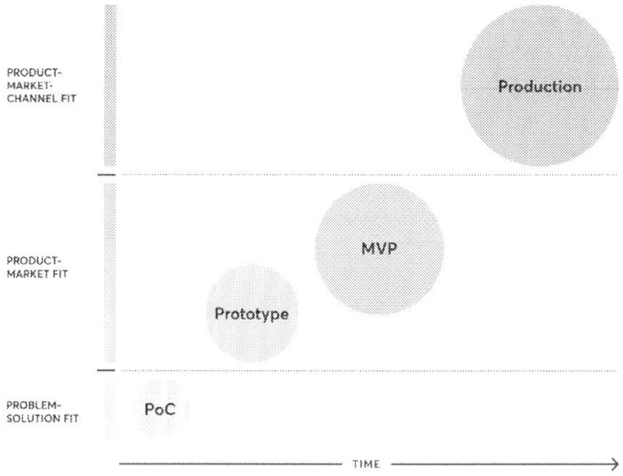

 69

Different stages of maturity

Two questions for each phase:

- What are the expected challenges?
- What are you looking to learn (or prove) in this phase?

 70

Proof-of-Concept challenges

Legal
Are you allowed to use the data?

Data
Is the data clean?

Does the data have relate/correlate to the problem?

Is the data representative of the real-world problem?

Technical
Is historical data available?

People
Are key stakeholders aligned with the PoC goals?

Do you have the right team and tools for execution?

Resource and Operational
Do costs and benefits match expectations?

Does time consumption match expectations?

Proof-of-Concept learnings

- ✓ Usability:
  - Does the proposed solution fit to the problem?
- ✓ Performance:
  - Comparison w.r.t. to a simple baseline, for example:
    - "Yesterday's weather" (last-known value)
    - Rest of the market
    - Averages/medians inside cluster
- ✓ Plan next steps:
  - If the baseline performance is comparable to a complex solution, implement the baseline instead! **The more explainable the solution, the higher the adoption rate.**
  - What is needed for a prototype?

Prototype challenges

Legal
Does the prototype comply with data privacy and security regulations?

Technical
Does your current tech stack support the prototype?

Usability
User friendly?

Does the user interface align with user expectations and needs?

Intiuitive?

People
Review by key stakeholders

Collaboration between development, design, and business teams?

Resource and Operational
Budget & time constraints

Required tools and infrastructure for building and testing?

 73

Prototype learnings

✓ Usability:
- Are end users able to do now what they couldn't do before?
- Does the user interface & experience (UI + UX) match expectations?
- Collect qualitative feedback on usability
- Iterate on this with a selected group of end users

✓ Performance:
- A/B testing between a test group and a control group: is there a significant **performance improvement** w.r.t. the business goal when using the prototype?
- Is the performance improvement large enough to **justify the costs** of an MVP or even full roll-out?

✓ Plan next steps:
- What is needed for an MVP?
- What is needed for a full roll-out?

 74

MVP challenges

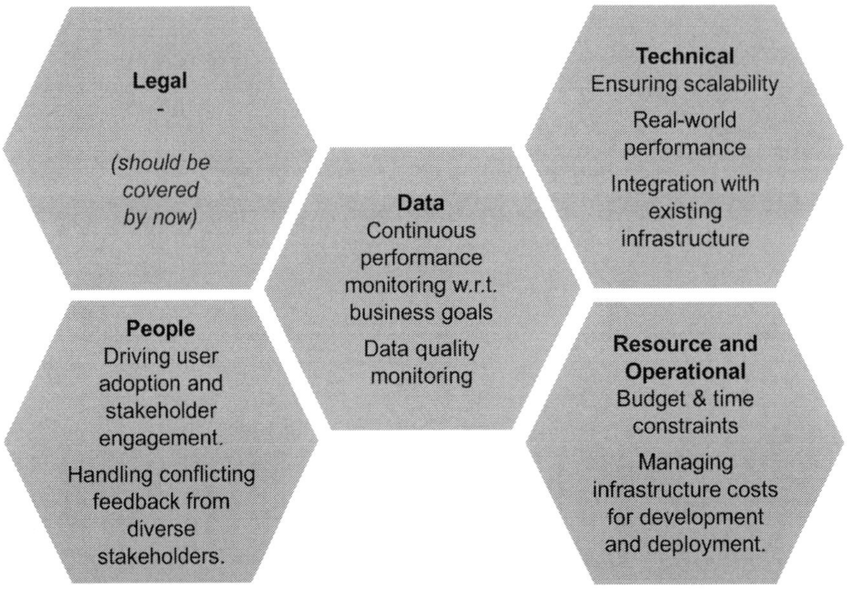

 75

MVP learnings

✓ Usability:
- Collect and address feedback on user experience gaps

✓ Performance:
- Measure system responsiveness
- Do the performance metrics from the PoC and prototype phase hold while rolling out the MVP for the rest of the group?
- Address any bottlenecks or inefficiencies

✓ Plan next steps:
- Prioritize features for the next iteration based on feedback
- Develop a roadmap for transitioning to a full production system
- Engage stakeholders to align on goals for the final product
- Prepare a detailed plan for scalability and maintenance

 76

Production challenges

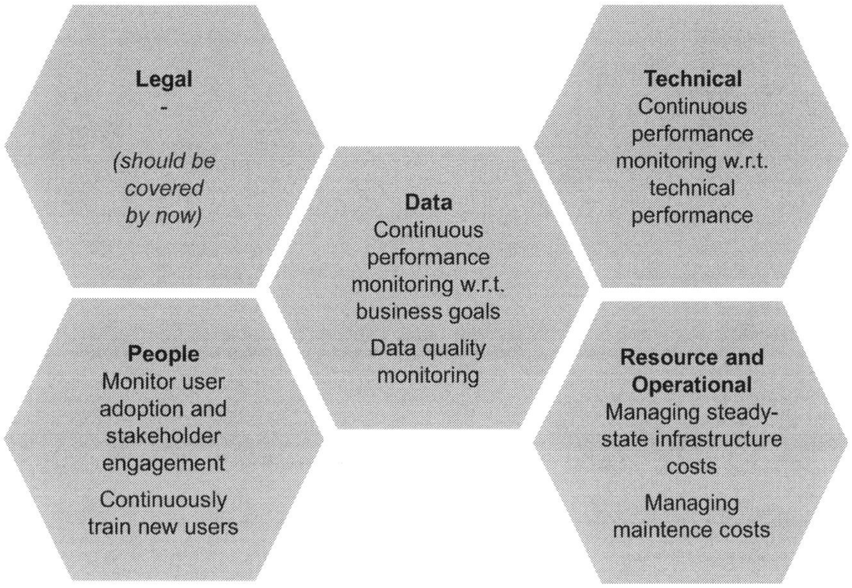

 77

Production learnings & steady-state maintenance

✓ Usability:
- Collect and address feedback on user experience gaps

✓ Performance:
- Measure system performance both from technical and business perspectives

✓ Plan next steps:
- Prioritize and plan creation of new features based on user requests
- Ensure proper governance & handovers
- Can the system be extended to facilitate easier roll-outs of new ideas?

 78

Implementation & Stakeholder Engagement

- First Steps in Implementation
- Engaging Stakeholders
- Establishing Insights
- Planning for Next Steps
- **Hands-on Workshop**

 79

Assignment: build your own engagement plan part 2

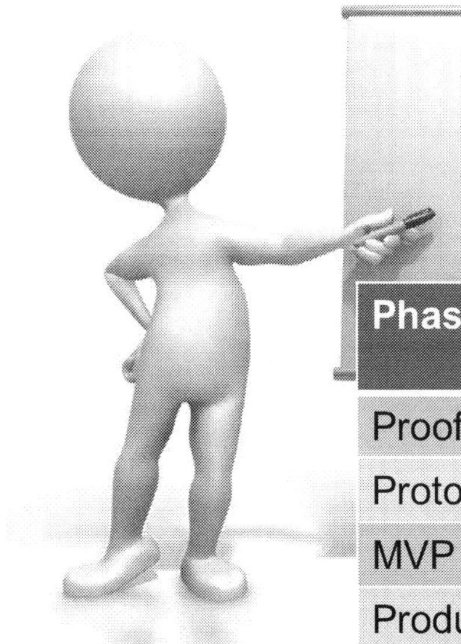

- ✓ Go back to your group of 3
- ✓ Take a big piece of paper
- ✓ Copy and fill the table below
- ✓ 10 minutes per phase

40 minutes

Phase	Challenges	Expected learnings
Proof-of-Concept		
Prototype		
MVP		
Production		

 80

Implementation &
Stakeholder
Engagement
• First Steps in Implementation
• Engaging Stakeholders
• Establishing Insights
• Planning for Next Steps
• Hands-on Workshop
© Van Haren Publishing
81

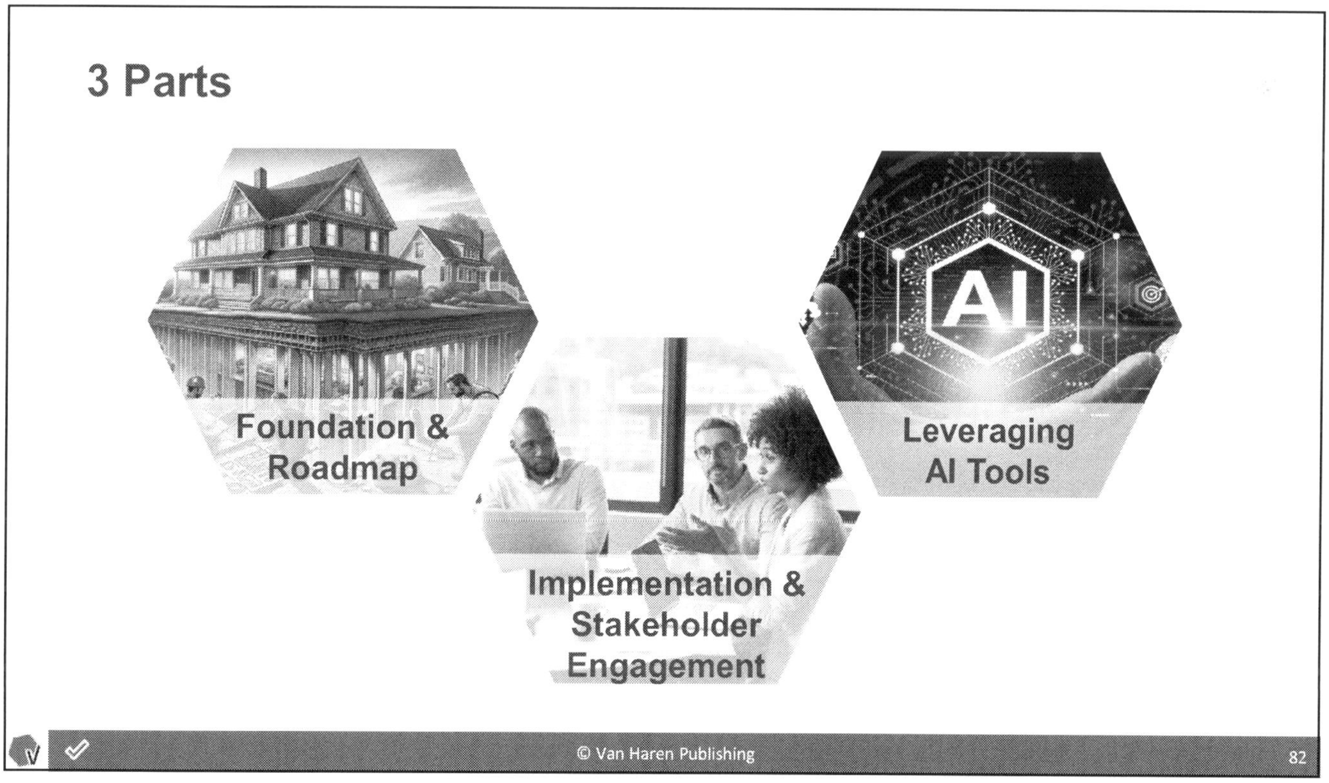
3 Parts
Foundation &
Roadmap
Implementation &
Stakeholder
Engagement
AI
Leveraging
AI Tools
© Van Haren Publishing
82

- **Introduction to AI Tools in Business**
- Hands-on Workshop with ChatGPT
- Deep Dive into Generative AI integration into your business
- Developing an Implementation Plan
- Next Steps and Q&A

 83

**“AI is booming,
we should be using it too!”**

 84

AI Tools in Business: narrow vs general AI

Narrow AI	General AI
Focused on a specific task	Capable of several different tasks
Image recognition Stock value prediction Breast cancer detection	Large-language models Image generation Video generation
Trained by data scientists, often inside the organization that uses the model	Created for a broad audience
Can predict or classify items based on a specific dataset	Can respond to any prompt
No self-awareness, values etc.	Values are typically built-in (eg what prompts are allowed, or how to respond to offensive prompts)

AI Tools in Business: narrow AI

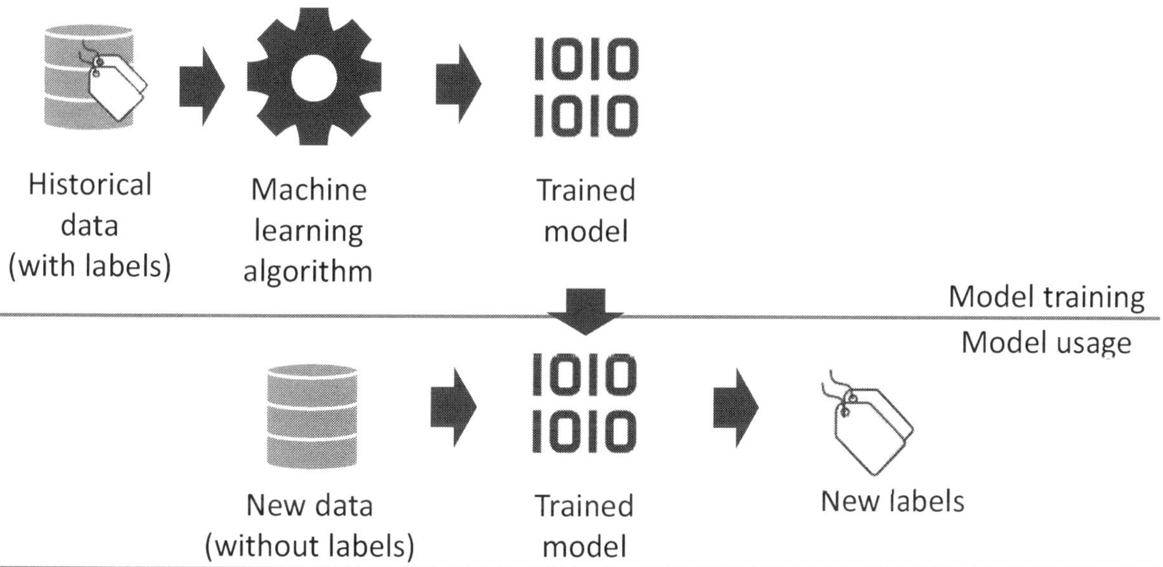

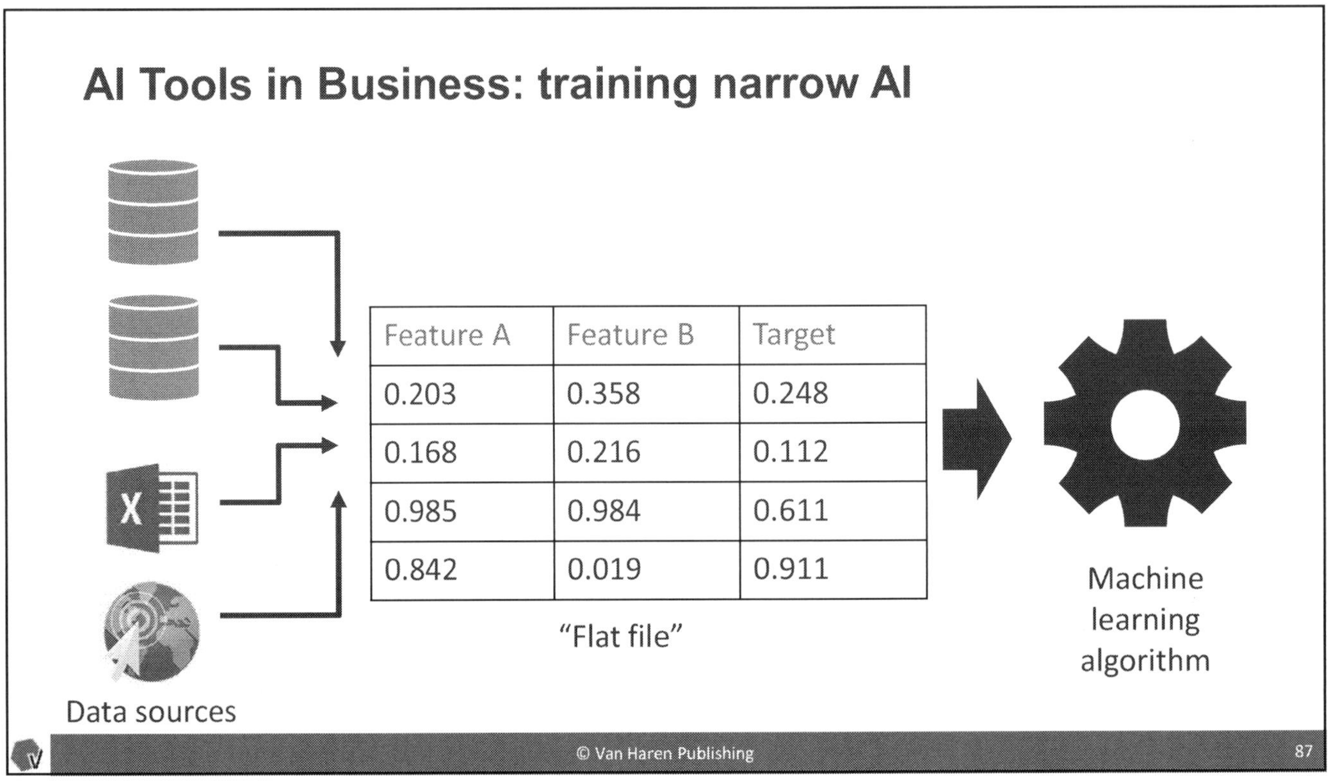

Feature A	Feature B	Target
0.203	0.358	0.248
0.168	0.216	0.112
0.985	0.984	0.611
0.842	0.019	0.911

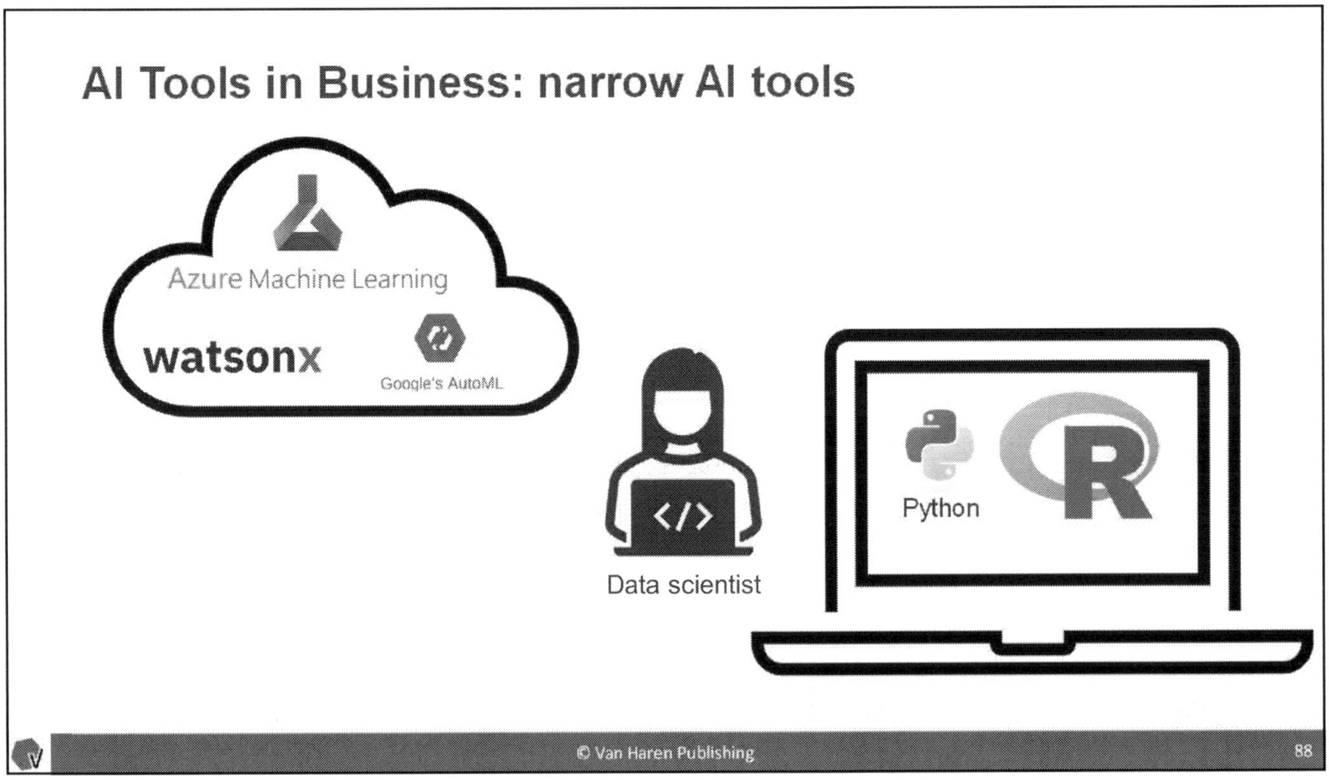

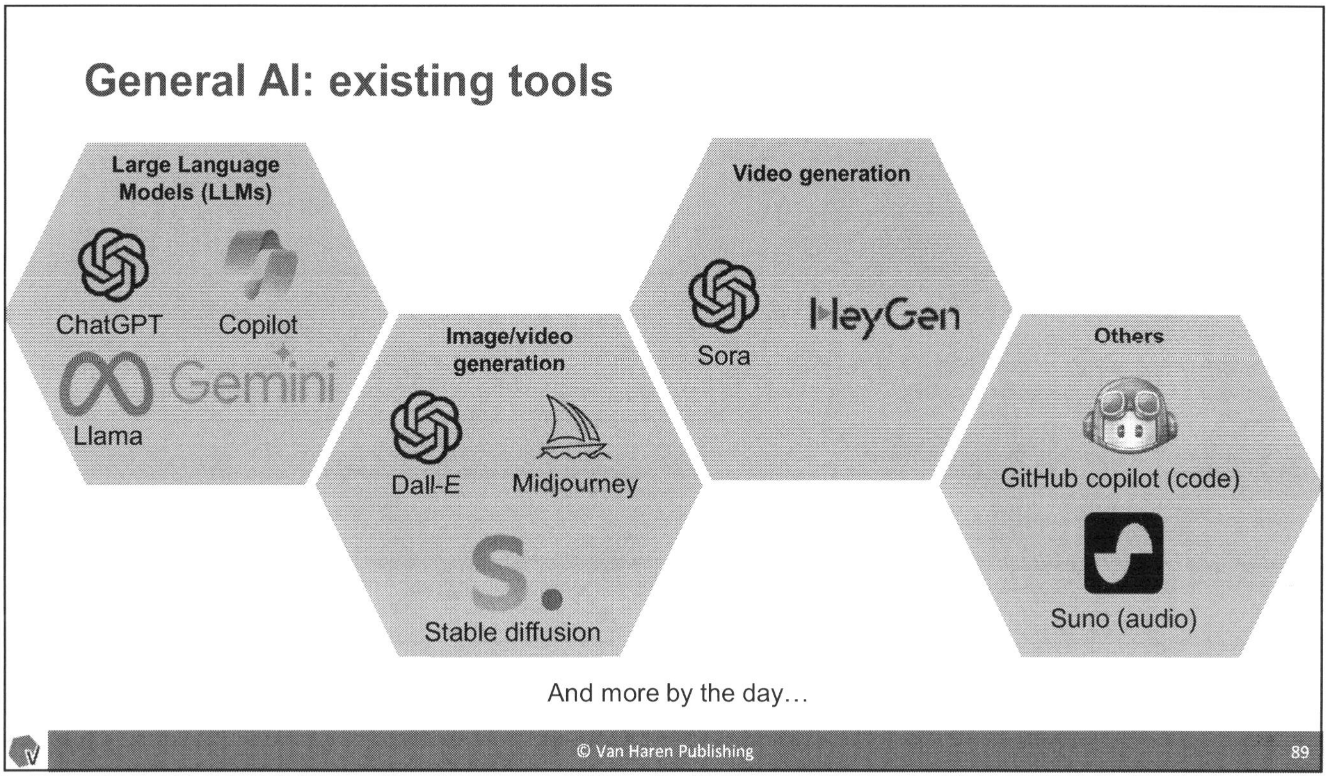
General AI: existing tools
Large Language Models (LLMs)
ChatGPT
Copilot
Gemini
Llama
Image/video generation
Dall-E
Midjourney
Stable diffusion
Video generation
Sora
HeyGen
Others
GitHub copilot (code)
Suno (audio)
And more by the day…
© Van Haren Publishing
89

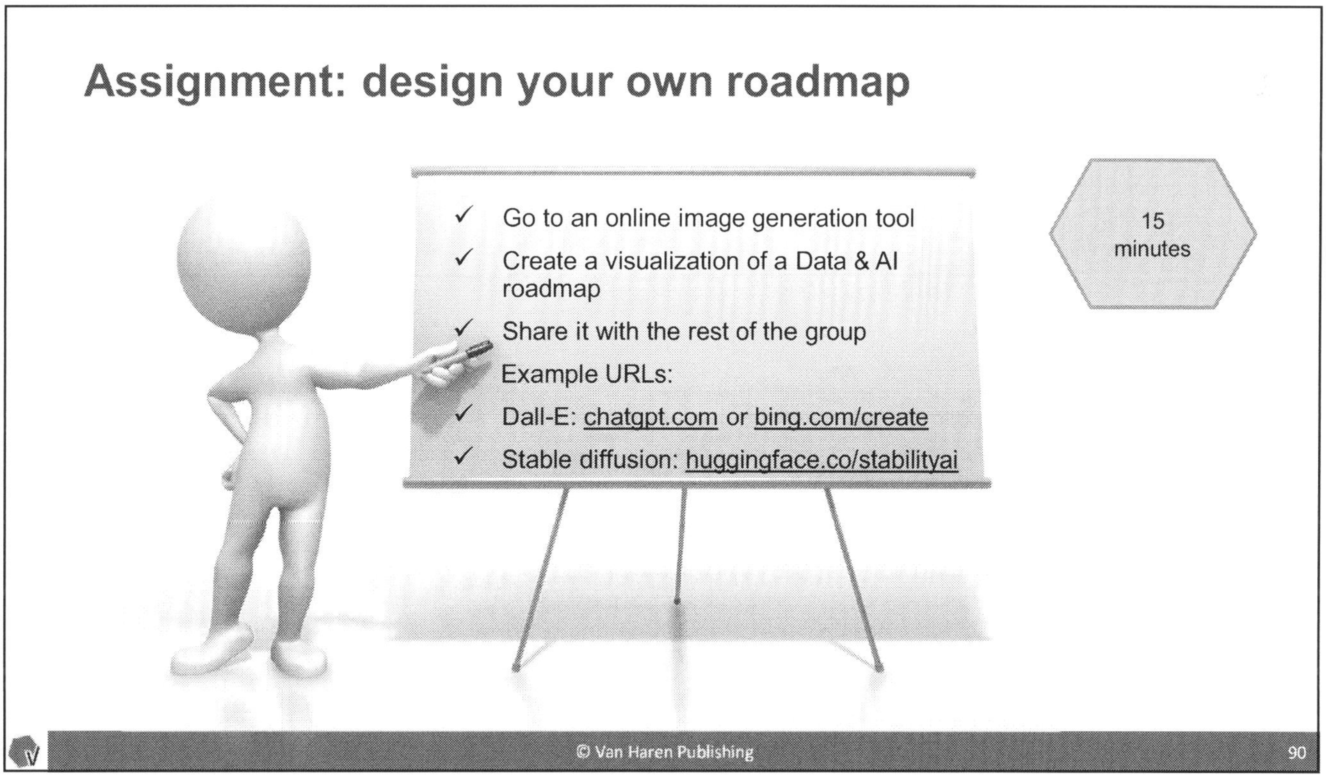
Assignment: design your own roadmap
✓ Go to an online image generation tool
✓ Create a visualization of a Data & AI roadmap
✓ Share it with the rest of the group
Example URLs:
✓ Dall-E: chatgpt.com or bing.com/create
✓ Stable diffusion: huggingface.co/stabilityai
15 minutes
© Van Haren Publishing
90

Sora

AI in business: narrow AI

✓ Narrow AI is used a lot for:
- (Stock) market predictions
- (Medical) image analysis
- Assortment recommendations
- Self-driving vehicles
- Recommender systems
- Fraud detection
- Translation
- Energy optimization
- Inventory management
- Cybersecurity
- Predictive maintenance
- Sentiment analysis
- Etc.

AI in business: LLMs

✓ Microsoft Copilot:
- Well-integrated in Microsoft Office
- Trusted as much as Microsoft Office
- Licensing model that facilitates data security
- Capable of generating a lot, but quality far from perfect

✓ ChatGPT:
- Used a lot as an assistant on the side, especially by people who have to generate text
- Quality of texts quite high
- Can be used to generate e-mail as well (through plugins)

✓ Llama
- Self-hostable: data security can be guaranteed
- Quality poor compared to above alternatives

 93

AI in business: image generation

✓ Dall-E, Midjourney
- No license fees required yet for Dall-E
- Very good at:
  - Artwork
  - Cartoon-like images
  - Initial designwork (dashboards, flyers, user interfaces, infographics)
- Not good at:
  - Factual images (words, numbers)
  - Correct infographics

✓ Stable diffusion
- Quality poor compared to other alternatives

 94

AI
Leveraging
AI Tools
• Introduction to AI Tools in Business
• Hands-on Workshop with ChatGPT
• Deep Dive into Generative AI integration into your business
• Developing an Implementation Plan
• Next Steps and Q&A
© Van Haren Publishing
95

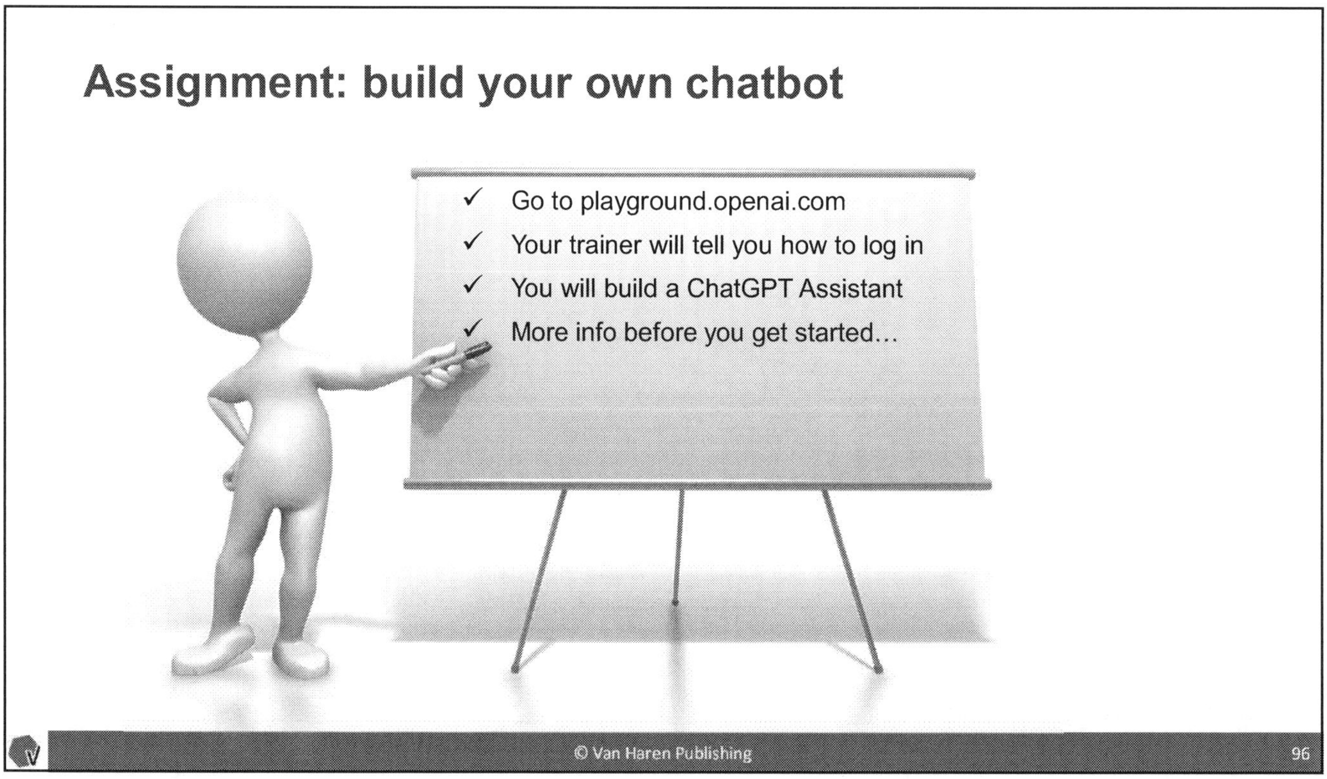
Assignment: build your own chatbot
✓ Go to playground.openai.com
✓ Your trainer will tell you how to log in
✓ You will build a ChatGPT Assistant
✓ More info before you get started…
© Van Haren Publishing
96

Hands-on Workshop with ChatGPT

- ✓ We will build a “Retrieval Augmented Generator” (RAG)
- ✓ This is ChatGPT, supplemented with files that it can use as input
- ✓ You can choose or generate your own dataset

Hands-on Workshop with ChatGPT

An example:

- ✓ Create a PDF with instructions of what to do in case a certain error occurs, with lines like:
  - When error 53 occurs, press 9
  - When error 65 occurs, press 7
- ✓ In the ChatGPT playground, go to Assistants

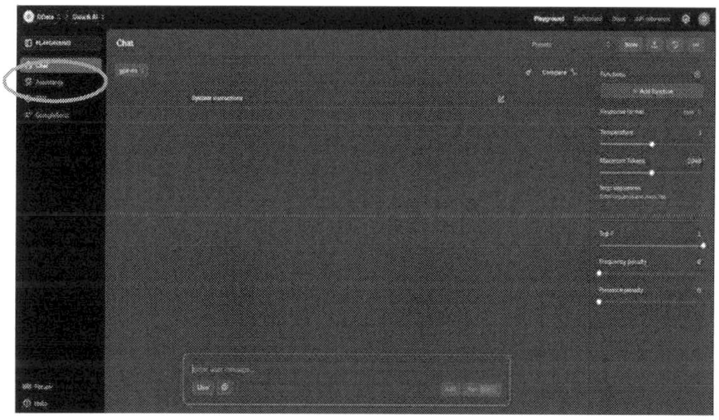

Hands-on Workshop with ChatGPT

An example:

- ✓ Create a PDF with instructions of what to do in case a certain error occurs, with lines like:
  - When error 53 occurs, press 9
  - When error 65 occurs, press 7
- ✓ In the ChatGPT playground, go to Assistants
- ✓ Upload your PDF here

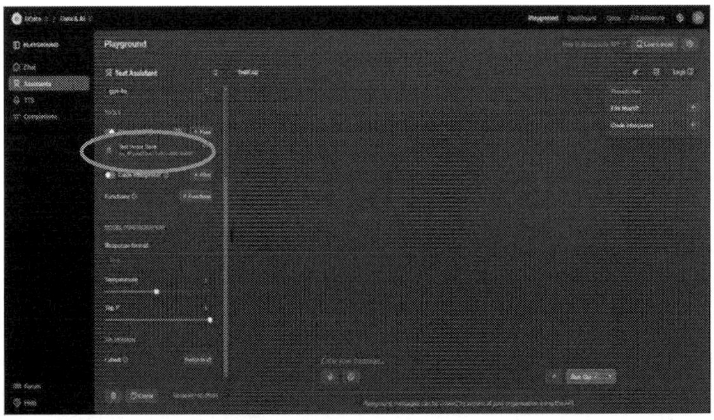

 99

Hands-on Workshop with ChatGPT

An example:

- ✓ Create a PDF with instructions of what to do in case a certain error occurs, with lines like:
  - When error 53 occurs, press 9
  - When error 65 occurs, press 7
- ✓ In the ChatGPT playground, go to Assistants
- ✓ Upload your PDF here
- ✓ Write a "System instruction", using AI. Make sure to ask it to always look in the file for the error code, and if it cannot find it, to answer that the specified error could not be found, and the user should contact the administrator.
- ✓ Play around to improve your chatbot

60 minutes

 100

- Introduction to AI Tools in Business
- Hands-on Workshop with ChatGPT
- **Deep Dive into Generative AI integration into your business**
- Developing an Implementation Plan
- Next Steps and Q&A

 101

Integrating generative AI into your business

1. Define Business Goals
2. Assess Data Readiness
3. Start with a Pilot Project
4. Develop and Deploy MVP
5. Scale and Optimize

 102

1. Define Business Goals

✓ Identify:
- your most time-consuming tasks
- your most expensive tasks
- your opportunities with the biggest potential

✓ Assess:
- Which of these are suitable for GenAI
- Should a human check the output first?
- What will the impact be on the business if:
  - the AI fails?
  - the AI succeeds?
  - the AI is down?
- Alternative solutions: do you really need GenAI?

Remember: not everything is an LLM problem!

 103

2. Assess Data Readiness

✓ Remember data quality:
- Accuracy
- Completeness
- Consistency
- Integrity
- Reasonableness
- Timeliness
- Uniqueness

✓ But also:
- Legality
- Privacy
- Ethics
- Risks

 104

3. Start with a Pilot Project

✓ With a small:
- data sample
- user group
- potentially customer group (eg: early adopters, or a launching customer)

✓ Build a proof-of-concept, showing:
- whether or not it works, based on pre-defined metrics (eg: speed, ease-of-use, etc)
- how much human oversight is required
- a cost indication of the project, maintenance and hosting/licensing

✓ Build a prototype:
- focus on the technical implementation and feasability
- pixel-perfectness comes later

 105

4. Develop and Deploy MVP

✓ Scale up:
- More users
- More customers
- Real-time integration into the infrastructure

✓ Focus on:
- User/customer adoption
- User/customer satisfaction
- Financial impact
- Other pre-defined KPIs
- Security

 106

5. Scale and Optimize

✓ Add more:
- Users
- Features

✓ Focus on:
- Decreasing maintenance
- Increasing efficiency
- Monitoring data streams
- Governance

Assignment: build your own GenAI integration plan

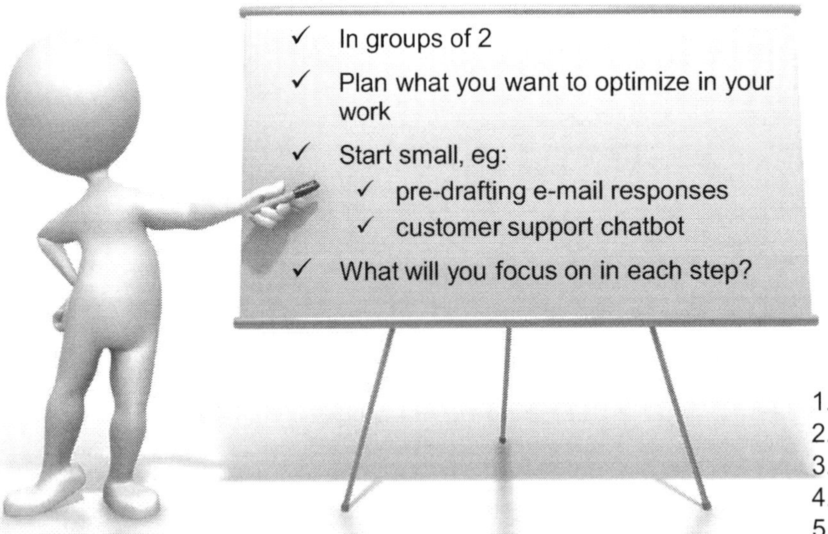

5x5 minutes

1. Define Business Goals
2. Assess Data Readiness
3. Start with a Pilot Project
4. Develop and Deploy MVP
5. Scale and Optimize

- Introduction to AI Tools in Business
- Hands-on Workshop with ChatGPT
- Deep Dive into Generative AI integration into your business
- **Developing an Implementation Plan**
- Next Steps and Q&A

© Van Haren Publishing 109

Developing an Implementation Plan

01
Gap analysis
- Tools
- Infrastructure
- Skills

02
Build a team
- IT
- Business
- Operations

03
Phased Roadmap
- PoC
- Prototype
- MVP
- Production

04
Secure resources
- Sponsorship
- Buy-in
- Technology
- Personnel

05
Measure success
- Define KPIs
- Review cycles

© Van Haren Publishing 110

Implementation Plan: Gap analysis

01
Gap analysis

- Tools
- Infrastructure
- Skills

- Identify current capabilities versus future needs
- Assess technical infrastructure readiness
- Determine gaps in data quality and availability
- Evaluate team skills and expertise
- Prioritize gaps to address first

 111

Developing an Implementation Plan

02
Build a team

- IT
- Business
- Operations

- Include IT, data scientists, and business leaders
- Assign ownership for key implementation areas
- Foster communication between technical and business stakeholders
- Define clear roles for execution and oversight
- Promote a culture of collaboration and accountability

 112

Developing an Implementation Plan

03
Phased Roadmap

- PoC
- Prototype
- MVP
- Production

- Outline short, medium, and long-term milestones
- Align phases with business priorities and resource availability
- Plan for early wins to demonstrate value quickly
- Incorporate feedback loops into each phase
- Ensure flexibility to adapt as needed

 113

Developing an Implementation Plan

04
Secure resources

- Sponsorship
- Buy-in
- Technology
- Personnel

- Prepare a strong business case with projected ROI
- Present clear benefits for stakeholders and end-users
- Allocate funding for technology and training
- Establish executive sponsorship for the strategy
- Ensure teams have adequate time and resources

 114

Developing an Implementation Plan

05
Measure success

- Define KPIs
- Review cycles

- Define KPIs to measure progress and outcomes
- Set up dashboards for real-time performance tracking
- Schedule regular review meetings to evaluate metrics
- Adjust implementation based on insights from monitoring
- Document lessons learned for future initiatives

 115

Developing an Implementation Plan

01
Gap analysis

- Tools
- Infrastructure
- Skills

02
Build a team

- IT
- Business
- Operations

03
Phased Roadmap

- PoC
- Prototype
- MVP
- Production

04
Secure resources

- Sponsorship
- Buy-in
- Technology
- Personnel

05
Measure success

- Define KPIs
- Review cycles

 116

- Introduction to AI Tools in Business
- Hands-on Workshop with ChatGPT
- Deep Dive into Generative AI integration into your business
- Developing an Implementation Plan
- **Next Steps and Q&A**

TODO

✓ TODO

- Introduction to AI Tools in Business
- Hands-on Workshop with ChatGPT
- Deep Dive into Generative AI integration into your business
- Developing an Implementation Plan
- Next Steps and Q&A

 119

3 Parts

 120

Made in United States
Orlando, FL
04 November 2026

90205814R00039